LEGO NINJAGO™

COMET CRISIS

#11 COMET CRISIS

GREG FARSHTEY • Writer
JOLYON YATES • Artist
LAURIE E. SMITH • Colourist

TITAN COMICS

LEGO® NINJAGO Masters of Spinjitzu
Volume 11: Comet Crisis

Greg Farshtey – Writer
Jolyon Yates – Artist
Laurie E. Smith – Colourist
Bryan Senka – Letterer

Published by Titan Comics, a division of Titan Publishing Group Ltd., 144 Southwark St., London, SE1 0UP. LEGO NINJAGO: VOLUME #11: COMET CRISIS. LEGO, the LEGO logo, the Brick and Knob configurations, the Minifigure and NINJAGO are trademarks of the LEGO Group ©2015 The LEGO Group. Produced under license from the LEGO Group. All rights reserved. All characters, events and institutions depicted herein are fictional. Any similarity between any of the names, characters, persons, events and/or institutions in this publication to actual names, characters, and persons, whether living or dead and/or institutions are unintended and purely coincidental. License contact for Europe: Blue Ocean Entertainment AG, Germany.

A CIP catalogue record for this title is available from the British Library.

Printed in China.

First published in the USA and Canada in January 2014 by Papercutz.

10 9 8 7 6 5 4 3 2 1

ISBN: 9781782762027

www.titan-comics.com

www.LEGO.com

MEET THE MASTERS OF SPINJITZU...

JAY

COLE

ZANE

KAI

And the Master of the
Masters of Spinjitzu...

SENSEI WU

THOUSANDS OF ASTEROIDS PASS NINJAGO EVERY YEAR, AND NO ONE GIVES THEM A SECOND THOUGHT.

AFTER ALL, THEY'RE JUST HUNKS OF SPACE ROCK, RIGHT?

"THAT WAS WHAT WE NINJA THOUGHT WHEN WE STOWED AWAY ON **GENERAL CRYPTOR'S** STARSHIP AND WOUND UP ON WHAT WE AT FIRST THOUGHT WAS A COMET, BUT TURNED OUT TO BE SOMETHING VERY DIFFERENT."

"CRYPTOR AND THE **NINDROIDS** HAD COME HERE IN SEARCH OF THE GOLD OF THE WEAPONS OF SPINJITZU AND THE MEGA WEAPON, AND WE TRIED TO STOP THEM."

"WE FAILED. CRYPTOR AND THE NINDROIDS ESCAPED, LEAVING US STRANDED WITH A BROKEN STARSHIP."

"WE WERE TRAPPED AND ALONE... OR SO WE THOUGHT."

WE HAD FORGOTTEN ONE THING:

AN ASTEROID TRAVELS THROUGH SPACE, AND ANYTHING THAT TRAVELS CAN CARRY...

A PASSENGER.

16

17

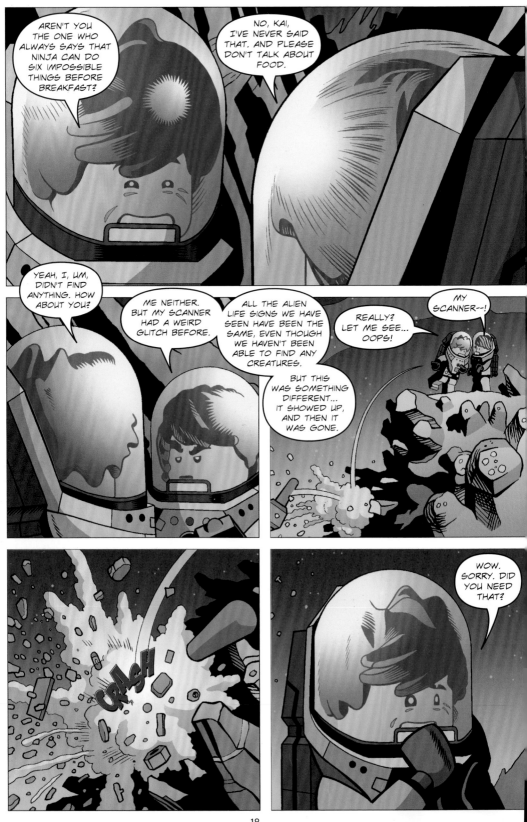

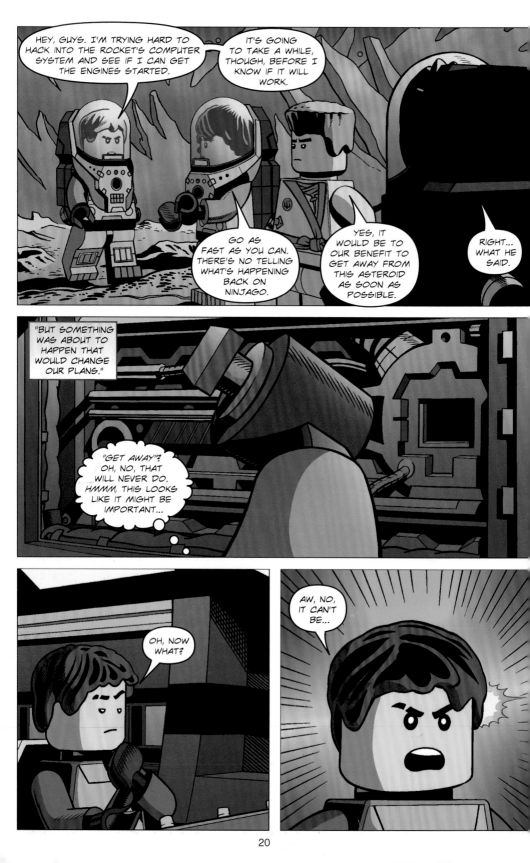

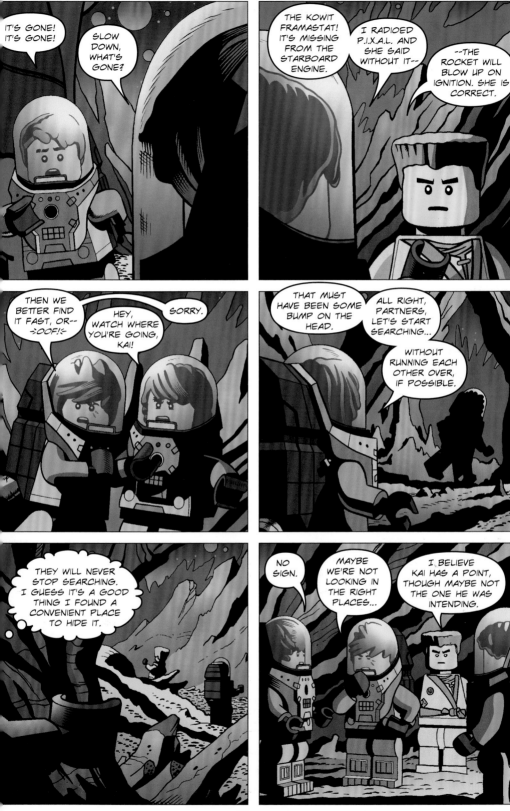

21

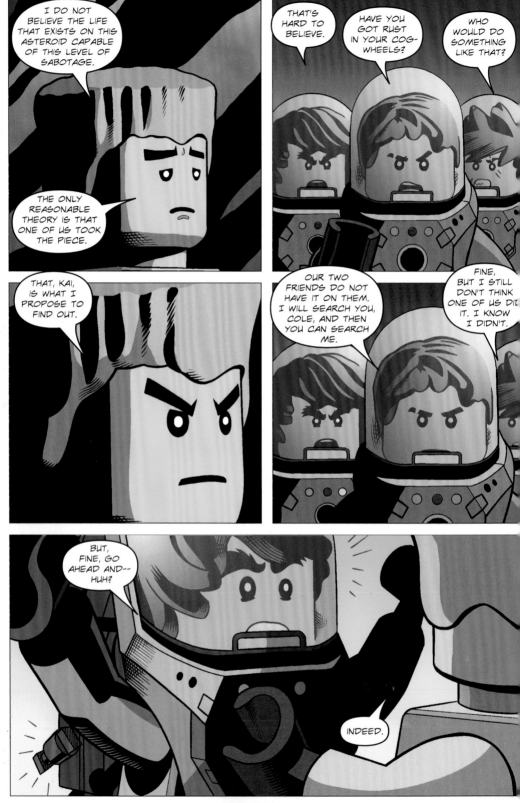

28

"ZANE, BEING LOGICAL, SUGGESTED THAT THE THREE OF US STAY AWAY FROM THE ROCKET AND ONLY JAY BE ALLOWED INSIDE.

"SINCE HE HAD DISCOVERED THE SABOTAGE, IT SEEMED UNLIKELY HE HAD BEEN THE ONE BEHIND IT."

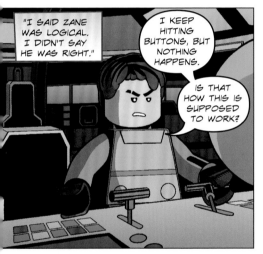

"I SAID ZANE WAS LOGICAL. I DIDN'T SAY HE WAS RIGHT."

I KEEP HITTING BUTTONS, BUT NOTHING HAPPENS.

IS THAT HOW THIS IS SUPPOSED TO WORK?

UH-OH...

SORRY, I GOT LOST OUT THERE. COLE CAME BACK, HUH?

JAY? HOW CAN YOU BE--?!

ALL OF YOU-- TO THE ROCKET! NOW!

AND WHO ARE YOU SUPPOSED TO BE?

NOT ME, I WOULD NEVER BUILD THIS PIECE OF JUNK!

IF YOU ARE GOING TO BE INSULTING--

--YOU'LL JUST HAVE TO GET OFF AND WALK.

YIPE.

HEY, IF YOU CRASH THIS THING, WHAT HAPPENS TO YOU?

ME? NOTHING. IN FACT, NOTHING EVER HAPPENS TO ME.

THAT'S THE PROBLEM.

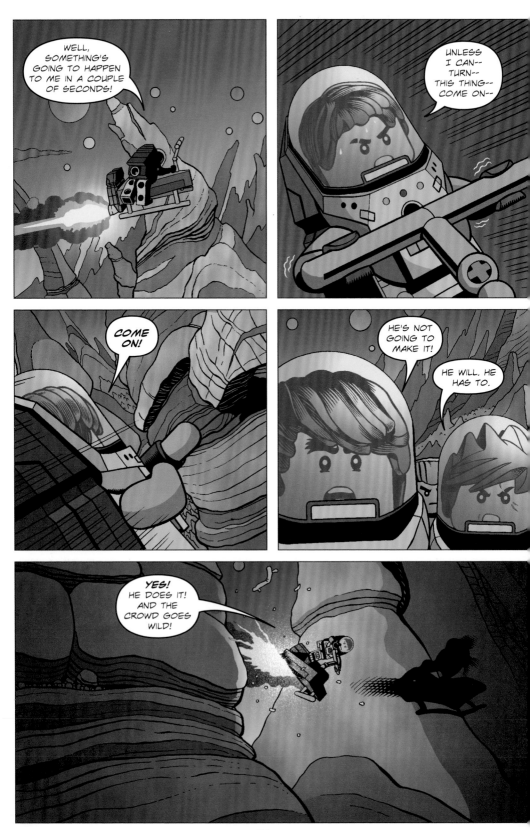

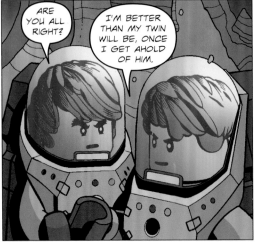

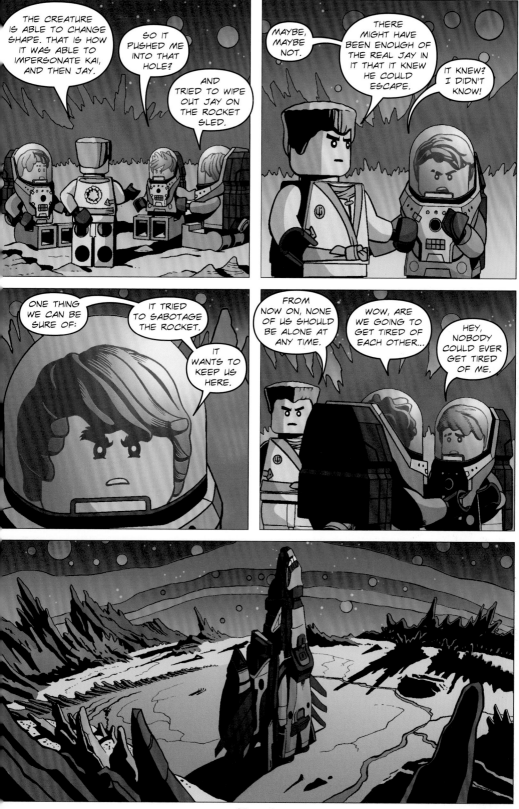

"JAY AND I TOOK FIRST WATCH. ZANE WAS MEDITATING IN THE ROCKET, AND KAI WAS IN THERE SLEEPING... BUT JAY WAS THE ONE ABOUT TO HAVE A NIGHTMARE."

COLE, IS THAT YOU?

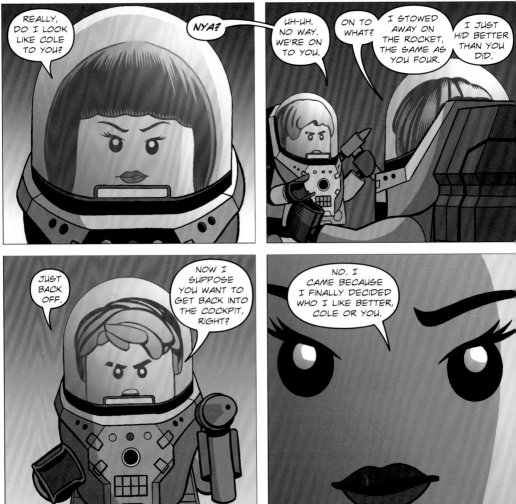

REALLY, DO I LOOK LIKE COLE TO YOU?

NYA?

UH-UH. NO WAY. WE'RE ON TO YOU.

ON TO WHAT?

I STOWED AWAY ON THE ROCKET, THE SAME AS YOU FOUR.

I JUST HID BETTER THAN YOU DID.

JUST BACK OFF.

NOW I SUPPOSE YOU WANT TO GET BACK INTO THE COCKPIT, RIGHT?

NO. I CAME BECAUSE I FINALLY DECIDED WHO I LIKE BETTER, COLE OR YOU.

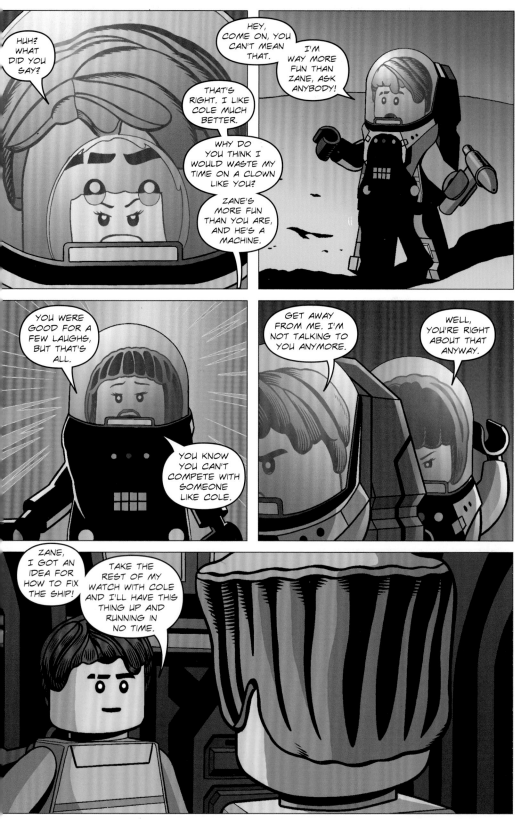

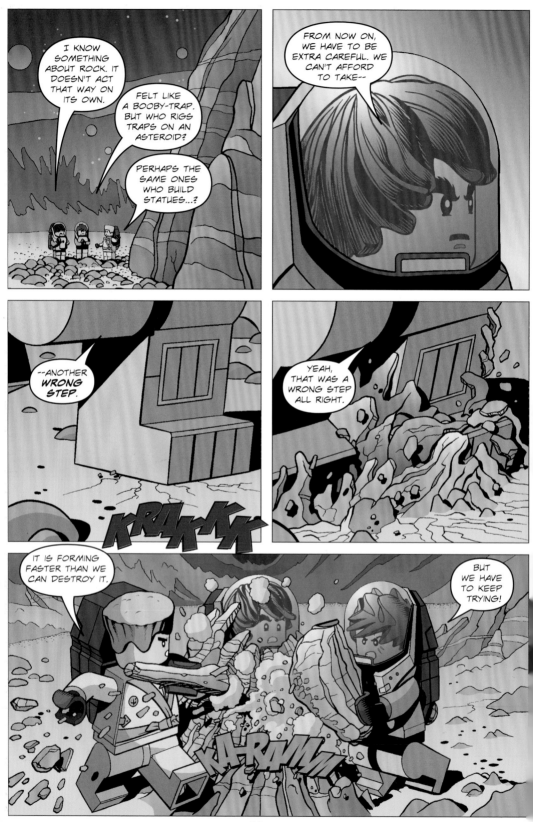

44

45

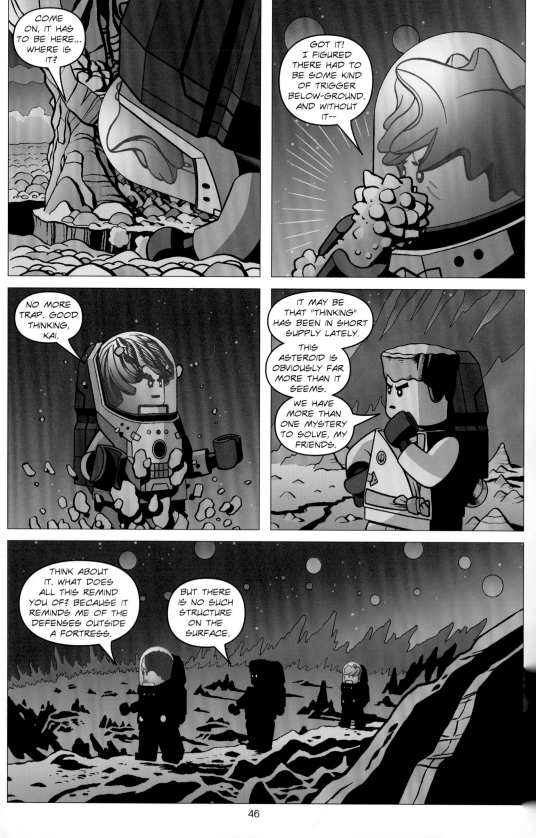

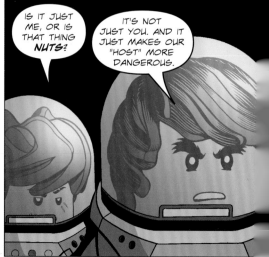

48

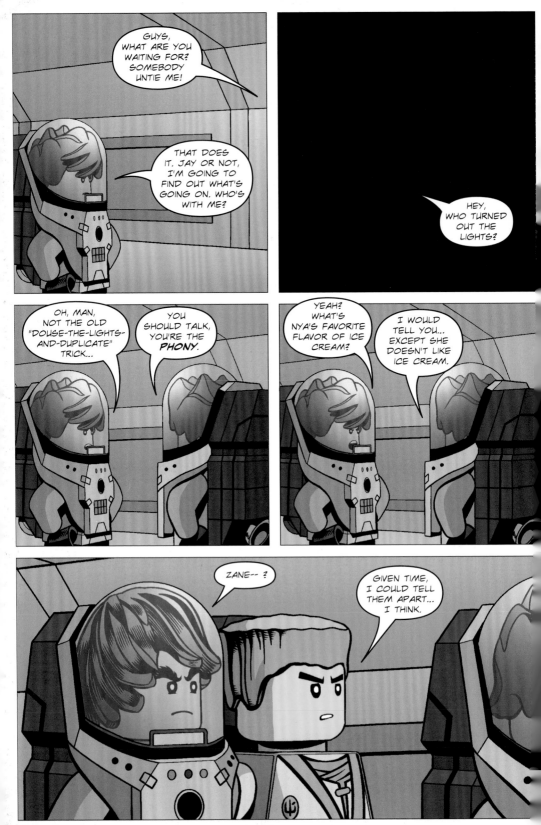

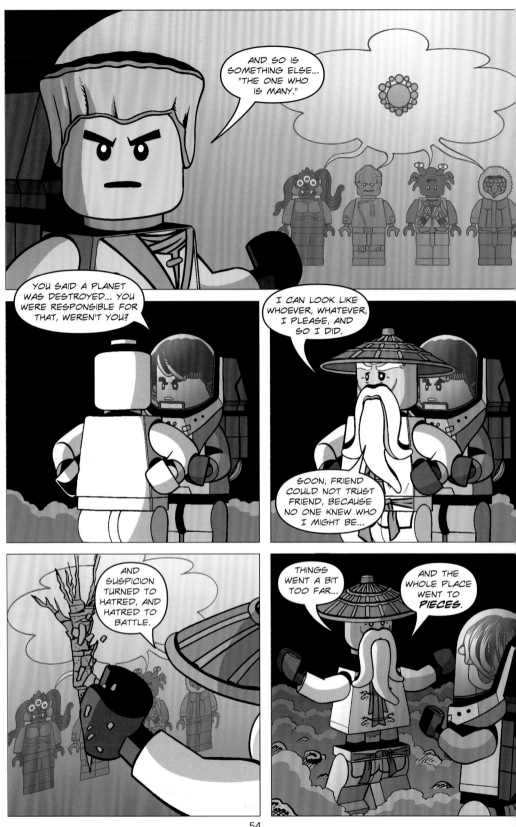

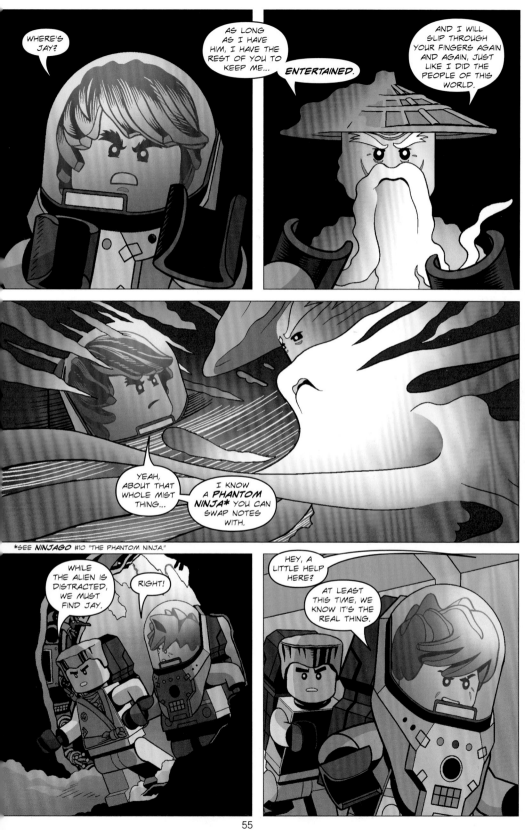

*SEE *NINJAGO* #10 "THE PHANTOM NINJA."

55

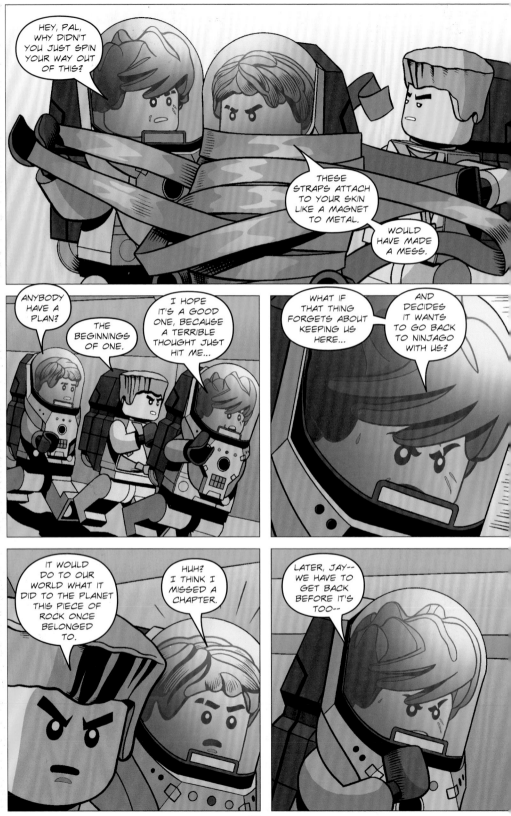

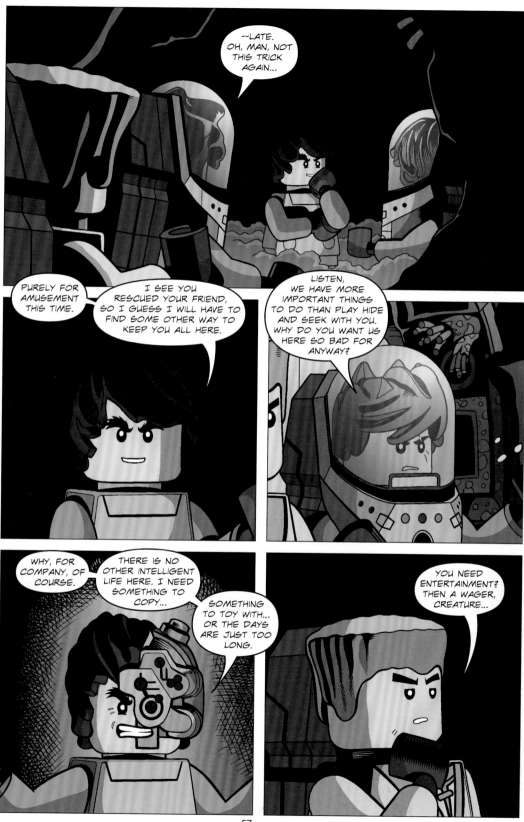

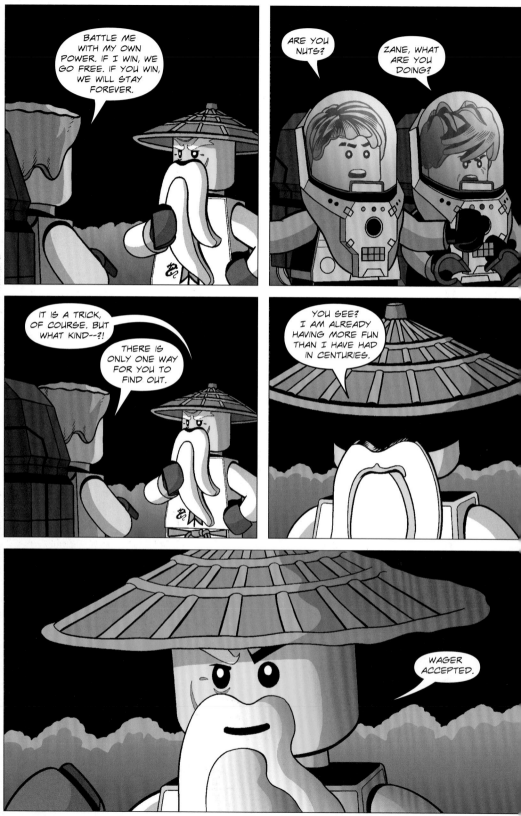

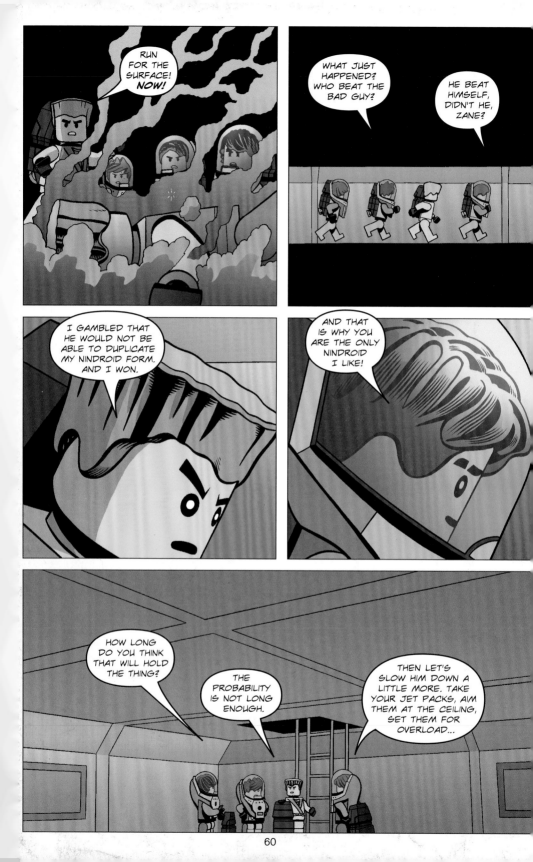

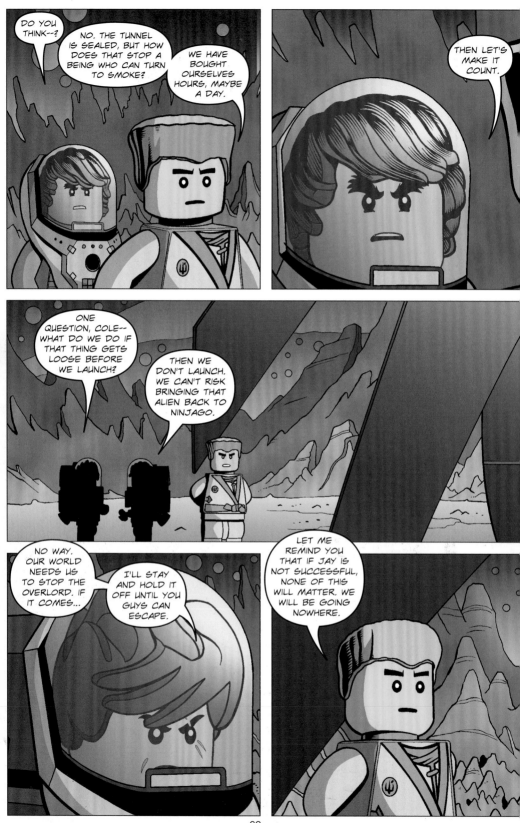

"WELL, AS IT TURNED OUT, JAY DIDN'T HAVE MUCH LUCK FIXING THE CONTROLS."

⊰YIIIII!⊱

ZZZAAKKK

"AND IT LOOKED FOR A WHILE LIKE WE WERE TO BE STUCK HERE A LONG, LONG TIME."

"BUT SOMEWHERE ALONG THE WAY, WE REMEMBERED WHO AND WHAT WE WERE... AND WE COMBINED OUR POWERS TO GET THE SHIP OFF THAT ROCK AND ON ITS WAY HOME."

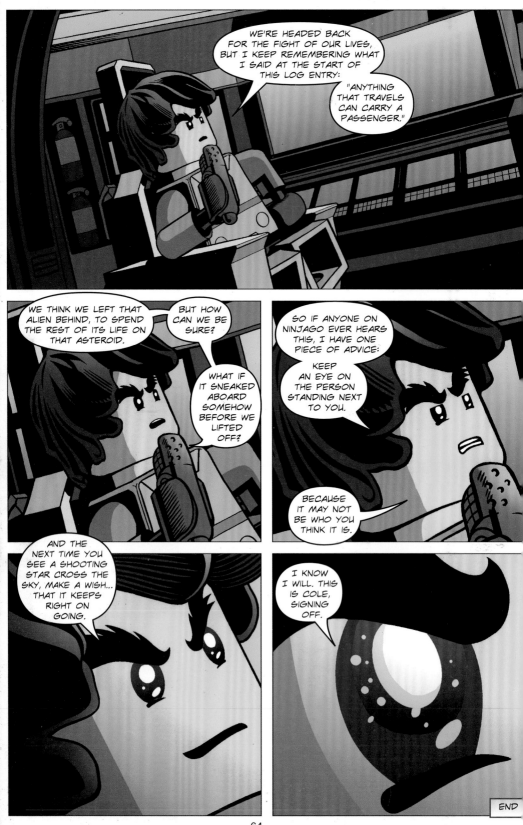